A WORLD OF RECIPES

Japan

REVISED AND UPDATED

Julie McCulloch

Heinemann
LIBRARY

www.heinemannlibrary.co.uk
Visit our website to find out more
information about Heinemann
Library books.

To order:

☎ Phone +44 (0) 1865 888066

▤ Fax +44 (0) 1865 314091

▣ Visit www.heinemannlibrary.co.uk

Heinemann Library is an imprint of Capstone Global Library
Limited, a company incorporated in England and Wales having
its registered office at 7 Pilgrim Street, London, EC4V 6LB
– Registered company number: 6695582

"Heinemann" is a registered trademark of Pearson Education
Limited, under licence to Capstone Global Library Limited

Edited by David Andrews and Diyan Leake
Designed by Richard Parker
Illustrated by Nicholas Beresford-Davis
Picture research by Mica Brancic
Originated by Chroma Graphics (Overseas) Pte Ltd
Printed and bound in China by Leo Paper Products Ltd

ISBN 978 0 431 11822 2 (hardback)
13 12 11 10 09
10 9 8 7 6 5 4 3 2 1

ISBN 978 0 431 11834 5 (paperback)
13 12 11 10 09
10 9 8 7 6 5 4 3 2 1

British Library Cataloguing in Publication Data
McCulloch, Julie, 1973-
  Japan. - 2nd ed. - (A world of recipes)
A full catalogue record for this book is available from the British
Library.

Acknowledgements
We would like to thank the following for permission to reproduce
photographs: Alamy p. **7** (Blend Images); © Capstone Global
Library Ltd/MM Studios pp. **36**, **37**; Corbis p. **5** (© Sakamoto
Photo Research Laboratory; Gareth Boden pp. **8–35**, **38–
43**;Photolibrary Group p. **6** (Corbis).

Cover photograph of assorted sushi reproduced with permission of
Photolibrary Group (Food Collection).

Every effort has been made to contact copyright holders of
material reproduced in this book. Any omissions will be rectified
in subsequent printings if notice is given to the publishers.

Disclaimer
All the Internet addresses (URLs) given in this book were valid at
the time of going to press. However, due to the dynamic nature of
the Internet, some addresses may have changed, or sites may have
changed or ceased to exist since publication. While the author and
publishers regret any inconvenience this may cause readers, no
responsibility for any such changes can be accepted by either the
author or the publisher.

Contents

Some words are shown in bold, **like this**. You can find out what they mean by looking in the glossary.

Japan

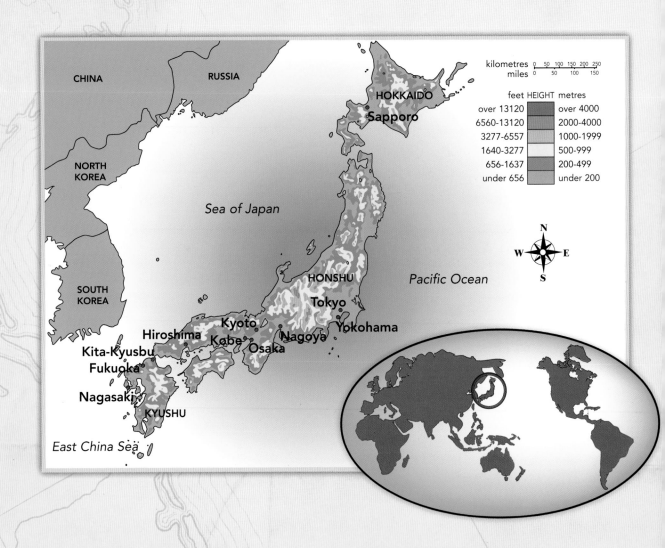

CHINA

RUSSIA

HOKKAIDO

Sapporo

NORTH KOREA

Sea of Japan

SOUTH KOREA

HONSHU

Pacific Ocean

Tokyo

Kyoto **Yokohama**

Hiroshima **Nagoya**

Kobe

Kita-Kyusbu **Osaka**

Fukuoka

Nagasaki

KYUSHU

East China Sea

kilometres 0 50 100 150 200 250
miles 0 50 100 150

feet HEIGHT metres

over 13120	over 4000
6560-13120	2000-4000
3277-6557	1000-1999
1640-3277	500-999
656-1637	200-499
under 656	under 200

N
W E
S

If you lived in Japan, you would never be more than 150 kilometres (90 miles) from the sea. Japan is a chain of over three thousand islands in the Pacific Ocean. High mountains, covered in trees, run down the center of the islands. Some of these mountains are active volcanoes. Cities are built along the flatter coasts.

Japan has a temperate climate with four seasons. Rainfall is heavy in spring and autumn, and summers are **humid**. Typhoons (tropical storms) often occur in the autumn.

In the past

The first people in Japan probably came from the mainland of Asia. By 1000 BC, people were growing rice they brought over from China.

Different clans and warlords fought for control of land. Since Japan has so many mountains, land for farming was scarce. The most powerful clan set up an imperial court similar to China's. The Buddhist religion and a form of writing were also introduced from China.

↑ This picture of a samurai warrior dates from around early in the 16th century.

Samurai warriors were the most important people in society from the 12th century onwards. Ordinary people were not allowed to carry weapons, but warriors carried two swords. A tax of rice was collected from ordinary people and given to the warriors. Samurais obeyed rules called *bushido*, meaning "the way of the warrior". For centuries, both emperors and shoguns (warrior leaders) ruled Japan.

Traders arrived from Portugal in the 16th century. The shoguns would not allow the traders to travel around the country. They made rules against trading with Europeans. Finally, Japan made a trading agreement with America in 1854. Japan adopted a Western style of government and legal system.

Japan today

Earthquakes are a threat in Japan. All new buildings are designed to survive a quake. Japanese children learn earthquake drills at school by hiding beneath their desks. Being in an earthquake zone does have its benefits, however. Hot springs are common in the country, and many people enjoy bathing in the warm waters.

Japanese food

Since Japan is surrounded by water, seafood is available everywhere. Edible seafood includes fish, fish eggs, squid and octopus, oysters, crabs, and sea urchins.

Sushi is an ancient Asian way of serving fish and rice together. The word *sushi* means "it's sour". From the 14th to 16th centuries, sushi rice was soured with vinegar.

Today, sushi rice is combined with different toppings and fillings. It may be wrapped in nori, seaweed that grows in the harbours. Nori is rolled into thin sheets and sun-dried before use. Sushi rice is also served with **sliced** raw fish.

Around the country

Over 70 percent of Japan is covered in mountains. Farmers find space for crops by planting on the mountainsides. Terraces (strips of flat land) are dug into the slopes. Each terrace is like a small field. Some mountains are terraced right to their tops.

Crops such as rice are grown on many of the terraces. On other terraces, wheat is grown in winter and vegetables are grown in summer.

← Rice fields in Japan stretch up the hills from the rocky shore.

An important fruit crop in the south is mandarin oranges. In the north, apples are grown. Soya beans are another important crop. They are used to make tofu, which is high in **protein**. They are also used to make a sauce that is used to flavour food.

Japanese meals

The same foods, usually including rice and a soup, are served three times each day. Rice is served with many small dishes that contain vegetables, fish, or meat. Pork and chicken are eaten much more than beef. Food is lightly cooked for a fresh taste. It is cut into bite-size pieces and eaten with chopsticks or fingers. Dessert is not usually served.

The tea ceremony

Tea was introduced by Buddhist monks in the 9th century. The traditional tea ceremony takes place in a tea house. When guests arrive, they bow. The tea is heated over a charcoal fire and poured into special drinking bowls. Guests wear kimonos (traditional robes) and sit on grass floor mats. They may eat a special meal that uses only fresh ingredients and is served on beautiful plates.

This picture ➜ shows two women in kimonos taking part in a tea ceremony.

Ingredients

Japanese cooking uses lots of ingredients which may be difficult to find outside Japan. You will find some in supermarkets, and some in oriental or health food shops. This book suggests alternatives for ingredients you may find hard to buy.

soy sauce

rice

egg noodles

tofu

sesame seeds

udon noodles

ginger

soba noodles

Dashi

Dashi is a liquid made from dried fish and seaweed. It is used in many dishes, but is difficult to find outside Japan. In this book we suggest using vegetable stock instead.

Ginger

Fresh ginger is used in many Japanese dishes, usually **peeled** and **grated**. It is readily available in supermarkets. It is better to use fresh rather than dried ginger, as it has more flavour.

Noodles

Noodles are very popular in Japan. There are many different types, but two of the most common types are soba (thin brown noodles) and udon (thick white noodles). These noodles are sometimes sold in supermarkets, but if you cannot get hold of them, use Chinese egg noodles, which are more widely available.

Rice

Rice is served at nearly every Japanese meal. There are two main types of rice – short grain and long grain. Short grain rice is closer to the type of rice used in Japan.

Seaweed

Seaweed is used in many Japanese dishes. There are many different types. Three of the most common are nori (black seaweed which is dried into sheets and used to wrap around rice, fish, and vegetables), kombu (dark green seaweed), and wakame (dark green seaweed which is used in soups and salads). Seaweed is not an essential ingredient in this book.

nori seaweed

Sesame seeds

Sesame seeds are used to flavour many different Japanese dishes. **Toasting** them brings out their full flavour.

Soy sauce

Soy sauce is made from soya beans, wheat, salt, and water. It is one of the most important ingredients in Japanese cooking, and is used in nearly every dish. It is called *shoyu* in Japanese.

Tofu

Also called bean curd, tofu is made from **pulped** soya beans. It can be found in most supermarkets.

Before you start

Which recipe should I try?

The recipes you choose to make depends on many things. Some recipes make a good main course, while others are better as starters. Some are easy, others are more difficult.

The top right-hand page of each recipe has information that can help you. It tells you how long each recipe will take and how many people it serves. You can multiply or divide the quantities if you want to cook for more or fewer people. This section also shows how difficult each dish is to make: the recipes are easy (*), medium (**), or difficult (***) to cook. The symbols in the corner can help you quickly find certain recipes. Here is a key that will help you.

 Healthy choice: These recipes are healthy to eat.

 Quick and easy: These recipes are quick and easy to make.

 Sweet treat: These recipes make a good dessert or sweet snack.

This symbol ⚠️ is sign of a dangerous step in a recipe. For these steps, take extra care or ask an adult to help.

Kitchen rules

There are a few basic rules you should always follow when you cook:

- Ask an adult if you can use the kitchen.
- Wash your hands before you start.
- Wear an apron to protect your clothes. Tie back long hair.
- Be very careful when using sharp knives.
- Never leave pan handles sticking out – it could be dangerous if you bump into them.

- Always wear oven gloves to lift things in and out of the oven.
- Wash fruit and vegetables before you use them.

Quantities and measurements

Ingredients for recipes can be measured in two different ways. Metric measurements use grams, litres, and millilitres. Imperial measurements use cups, ounces, and fluid ounces. In the recipes in this book you will see the following abbreviations:

tbsp = tablespoons   oz = ounces
tsp = teaspoons   ml = millilitres
g = grams   cm = centimetres

Utensils

To cook the recipes in this book, you will need these utensils, as well as kitchen essentials, such as forks, spoons, plates, and bowls.

- chopping board
- **colander**
- food processor or blender
- frying pan
- grater
- heatproof bowl
- large, flat, ovenproof dish
- measuring jug
- rolling pin
- saucepan with lid

- set of scales
- sharp knife
- skewers
- steamer or roasting tin
- wok (if you don't have a wok, you can use a large frying pan instead)
- whisk
- wooden spoon

Clear soup

Many Japanese people eat a bowl of soup for breakfast, or at the beginning of a formal meal. It is not eaten with a spoon – the idea is to pick out the solid ingredients with chopsticks, then pick up the bowl and drink the liquid.

What you need

½ carrot

1 spring onion

100g tofu

800ml water

50g udon noodles
(or Chinese egg
noodles)

1 vegetable stock cube

1 tbsp soy sauce

½ tbsp granulated
sugar

What you do

1 **Peel** the carrot, and cut it into thin **slices**.

2 Cut the top and bottom off the spring onion, and finely **chop** it.

3 Cut the tofu into small pieces, about 1cm across.

4 Put the water into a saucepan, and bring it to the **boil**. Slowly lower the noodles into the water. Turn the heat down, and leave the noodles to **simmer** for 4 minutes, until they are soft.

5 **Drain** the water from the noodles using a **colander**. Put them into the bottom of two small bowls.

6 Put 500ml water into a saucepan, and bring it to the boil. Crumble the stock cube into the water, and stir until it **dissolves**. Turn the heat down to a simmer.

7 Add the sliced carrot, chopped spring onion, tofu pieces, soy sauce, and sugar to the stock.

8 Simmer the stock for 5 minutes.

9 Carefully pour the stock over the noodles, and serve.

ADDED EXTRAS

You can add many different ingredients to clear soup.
Try adding a small amount of the following:

- sliced mushrooms
- spinach
- mangetout
- prawns

You can also add wakame seaweed to clear soup, if you can find some. You need to stand the wakame in cold water for about 20 minutes, until it is soft. Then cut it into strips about 1cm wide, and put it in the bottom of the bowl with the noodles.

Savoury custard

This savoury custard is a bit like a thick soup, and is called *chawan mushi* in Japanese. It might be served at the end of a meal, or as a snack. It is usually eaten hot, but is sometimes served cold during the hot summer months.

What you need

225ml water
1 vegetable stock cube
¼ tbsp granulated sugar
½ tbsp soy sauce
2 eggs

What you do

1. Put the water into a saucepan, and bring it to the **boil**. Crumble the stock cube into the water, and stir until it **dissolves**. Turn the heat down to a **simmer**.

2. Add the sugar and soy sauce to the stock. Stir until the sugar dissolves.

3. Leave the stock to **cool** for about 15 minutes.

4. While the stock is cooling, crack the eggs into a bowl. **Beat** them with a fork or a whisk until the yolk and the white are mixed.

5. Pour the beaten eggs into the cooled stock, stirring gently as you pour.

6. Carefully pour the custard into two ramekin dishes.

7. Put the ramekin dishes in a steamer. Place the steamer over a pan of boiling water.

8 Turn the heat down to low. Put the lid on the steamer. **Steam** the custards for 30 minutes, until the mixture is set.

  9 Wear an oven glove to remove the hot ramekins from the steamer. Serve your custards in these dishes.

COOKING IN THE OVEN
If you don't have a steamer, you can cook your custards in the oven. Preheat the oven to 220°C/425°F/gas mark 7. Half-fill a roasting tin with hot water, and place the ramekins full of custard in the water. Cover the whole roasting tin with foil. Put the tin in the oven, and cook the custards for 30 minutes.

TRY HUNTING!
Try adding other ingredients, such as mushrooms or prawns, to the basic custard, at stage 5. You can hunt for the different ingredients when you eat the custard!

Grilled tofu

The main religion in Japan is Buddhism. Buddhist temples often contain small restaurants, serving **vegetarian** food. Many of these dishes are based on tofu. This grilled tofu dish is typical of the sort of food served in temples. You could serve it as a starter or a snack.

What you need

150g tofu
1 tbsp soy sauce
1 tbsp granulated
    sugar
1 tbsp lemon juice
1 tbsp sesame seeds

What you do

1 Cut the tofu into 8 pieces, about 1cm thick.

2 Put the soy sauce, sugar, and lemon juice into a bowl. Add the tofu pieces, and leave them to **marinate** for about an hour.

3 If you are using wooden skewers, soak them in water.

4 While the tofu is marinating, put the sesame seeds into a frying pan without adding any oil. Heat the seeds over a medium heat for about 5 minutes, keeping the pan moving, until they are golden brown. Some may pop out, so stand back! Put the **toasted** sesame seeds to one side.

5 When the tofu pieces are marinated, thread them onto skewers.

6 Turn the grill on to a medium heat. **Grill** the tofu pieces on their skewers for 3 minutes on each side, until they are a golden brown colour, and cooked through.

Ready to eat: 1 hour 10 minutes (including 1 hour to marinate the tofu).
Difficulty: *. Serves 2.

 7 **Sprinkle** the toasted sesame seeds over the tofu. Wait for the skewers to **cool** a little. Serve with a little dish of soy sauce to dunk the tofu in. Keep the tofu on the skewers, and nibble it off!

LOLLY STICKS

If you don't have skewers, you can grill the tofu on wooden lolly sticks, which you can buy from most supermarkets. Soak the lolly sticks in water for 10 minutes before using them so they will not burn under the grill.

Grilled chicken

This grilled chicken dish is called *yakitori* in Japanese. Yakitori bars – small restaurants which only serve this dish – are found all over Japan.

What you need

- 2 chicken breasts
- 1 tbsp soy sauce
- ½ tbsp granulated sugar

What you do

1 If you are using wooden skewers, soak them in water.

2 Cut the chicken breasts into 2cm cubes.

3 Mix the soy sauce and sugar in a large, flat dish, and put the chicken pieces into the sauce. **Marinate** the chicken in the sauce for about an hour.

4 Thread the chicken pieces on to skewers.

5 Turn the grill on to a medium heat. **Grill** the marinated chicken pieces on their skewers for about 15 minutes. Halfway through, remove them from the grill. Wearing an oven glove, turn them and grill until golden brown and cooked through.

Ready to eat: 1 hour 25 minutes (including 1 hour to marinate the chicken).
Difficulty: *. Serves 2.

VEGETARIAN SKEWERS

You could use vegetables instead of, or as well as, chicken in this dish. Try pieces of courgette, mushroom, or red pepper as shown in the photo below. You could cook them outside on a barbecue in the summer.

Chicken soup

This soup is served as a main course in Japan. As with the clear soup on page 12, you eat the solid ingredients with chopsticks, then drink the liquid from the bowl.

What you need

250g udon noodles (or Chinese egg noodles)

1 vegetable stock cube

2 tbsp soy sauce

2 tbsp granulated sugar

2 chicken breasts

600ml water

4 spring onions

What you do

1 Mix the soy sauce and sugar in a large, flat bowl.

2 Put the chicken breasts into the soy sauce and sugar mixture. Turn them over a couple of times until they are coated. Leave the chicken to **marinate** in the sauce for about an hour.

3 When the chicken has marinated, turn the grill on to a medium heat. **Grill** the marinated chicken for about 15 minutes, turning halfway through, until it is golden brown and cooked through.

4  Using a fork to lift it, carefully take the chicken out of the grill. Cut it into **slices**, using a sharp knife. Put them to one side.

Ready to eat: 1 hour 40 minutes (including 1 hour to marinate the chicken).
Difficulty: **. Serves 2.

5 Put the water into a saucepan, and bring it to the **boil**. Crumble the stock cube into the water, and stir until it **dissolves**.

6 Add the noodles to the hot stock. Boil them for about 5 minutes, until they are soft.

7 Cut the tops and bottoms off the spring onions and throw them away. Finely **chop** the spring onions.

8 Pour the noodles and stock into two bowls. Arrange the chicken slices and the chopped spring onions on top of the noodles, then serve the soup.

Prawn and vegetable stir-fry

Food that is stirred while it is being fried over a high heat makes a dish called a **stir-fry**. The ingredients in this traditional stir-fry are cooked very quickly, so the vegetables should still taste crunchy.

What you need

½ courgette
60g mushrooms
2 spring onions
½ tbsp sunflower oil
150g prawns
100g bean sprouts
½ tbsp lemon juice
1 tbsp soy sauce

What you do

1 Cut the courgette and the mushrooms into **slices**.

2 Cut the tops and bottoms off the spring onions, and finely **chop** them.

3 Heat the oil in a frying pan.

4 Put the sliced courgette and mushrooms, prawns, and bean sprouts into the frying pan. **Fry** the ingredients on a high heat, stirring continuously, for about 5 minutes.

5 Add the chopped spring onion, lemon juice, and soy sauce to the frying pan, and cook for another 2 minutes before serving.

MORE STIR-FRY IDEAS

You could adapt this recipe to use all sorts of different ingredients. Try replacing the mushrooms and courgette with other vegetables, such as:

- sliced carrots
- sliced mushrooms
- mangetout
- pieces of broccoli

Chilled noodles

In parts of Japan where summers are very hot, noodles are sometimes served cold. Dip each mouthful of noodles into the sauce before you eat it.

What you need

1 spring onion
450ml water
1 vegetable stock
  cube
50ml soy sauce
1 tbsp granulated
  sugar
100g soba noodles
  (or Chinese egg
  noodles)

What you do

1 Cut the top and bottom off the spring onion and throw them away. Finely **chop** the spring onion.

2 Put 150ml water in a saucepan, and bring it to the **boil**. Crumble the stock cube into the water, and stir until it **dissolves**.

3 Add the soy sauce, sugar, and spring onion to the stock. **Simmer** the sauce for a couple of minutes until the sugar has dissolved.

4 Carefully pour the sauce into two small dishes, and leave to **cool**.

5 Put 300ml water into a pan and bring it to the boil. Add the noodles, and cook them for about 5 minutes, until they are soft.

6 Tip the noodles into a **colander**. **Rinse** them in cold water and put them into two small dishes.

7 Give each person a dish of noodles and a dish of sauce.

HOW TO USE CHOPSTICKS

Pick up one chopstick, and hold it between your thumb and first two fingers. This chopstick is the one that will move.

Put the second chopstick between your second and third fingers, and behind your thumb. This chopstick stays still. Move the top chopstick up and down with your thumb and first finger so that the tips of the chopsticks meet.

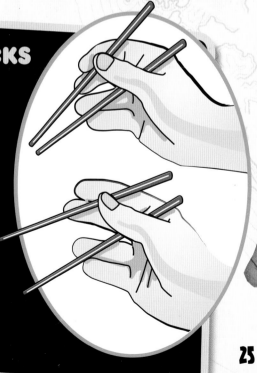

Salmon teriyaki

Teriyaki is the Japanese name for a sauce made from soy sauce and sugar. Teriyaki sauce can be eaten with many different ingredients, such as fish, chicken, tofu, and vegetables. In this dish, it goes well with salmon.

What you need

1 tbsp sunflower oil
2 salmon steaks
100g mushrooms
50g bean sprouts
50ml soy sauce
1 tbsp granulated
   sugar

What you do

1 **Slice** the mushrooms.

2 Put the soy sauce, sugar, and 2 tbsp water into a saucepan. Bring the mixture to the **boil**, then **simmer** for about 10 minutes, stirring regularly, until the sauce is thick and syrupy.

3 Take the pan off the heat, and put a lid on it to keep the sauce warm.

4 Heat the oil in a frying pan, and add the sliced mushrooms and bean sprouts. **Fry** them for about 5 minutes, then put them into an ovenproof dish.

5 Turn the oven on to its lowest setting, and put the vegetables into the oven to keep warm.

6 Put the salmon steaks into the frying pan. Cook them for about 5 minutes on each side, until they are slightly brown and cooked through.

7 Put one salmon steak and some of the cooked vegetables onto each plate. Carefully spoon the sauce over the salmon.

Beef tataki

For this dish, the beef needs to **marinate** so that it can soak up all the flavours of the sauce. Start making it well before you want to eat it!

What you need

225g steak
1 onion
½ tbsp lemon juice
50ml white wine vinegar (or malt vinegar)
50ml soy sauce
1 tbsp granulated sugar
Lettuce leaves

What you do

1. Turn the grill on to a medium heat. **Grill** the steak for 15 minutes, turning halfway through so that both sides are cooked.

2. While the steak is cooking, **peel** the onion and finely **chop** half of it.

3. Cut the steak in half to check that it is cooked all the way through, not still red.

4. Mix together the chopped onion, lemon juice, white wine vinegar, soy sauce, and sugar in a bowl. Add the steak, and coat it well with the marinade.

5. Leave the steak to marinate for at least 3 hours.

6. Remove the steak from the marinade. Cut it into thin **slices**.

Ready to eat: 3 hours 30 minutes (including 3 hours to marinate the meat). Difficulty: **. Serves 2.

 7 Arrange the lettuce leaves on plates, and place the beef slices on top.

EATING MEAT

Meat is thought of as quite a luxury in Japan, as it is very expensive. It is usually cut into thin slices and served with vegetables or salad, as in this dish.

Steamed chicken with broccoli

Most Japanese cooking is very healthy. This steamed chicken is particularly good for you, because it does not contain any fat.

What you need

2 chicken breasts
50ml soy sauce
½ tbsp granulated sugar
75g broccoli

What you do

1 Mix the soy sauce and sugar in a bowl. Put the chicken into the bowl, and leave to **marinate** for about an hour, turning once so that all the chicken is coated with the marinade.

2 Put the marinated chicken into a steamer over a saucepan of boiling water. Turn the heat down to low. **Steam** for 15 minutes, then turn the chicken over and steam for another 10 minutes.

3 Meanwhile, **chop** the broccoli into small pieces.

4 Bring a saucepan of water to the **boil**. Add the broccoli, and cook for 5 minutes.

5 Carefully take the chicken breasts out of the steamer, using a fork to lift them. Put them onto a chopping board. **Slice** them into pieces about 5mm thick.

Ready to eat: 1 hour 35 minutes (including 1 hour to marinate the chicken). Difficulty: **. Serves 2.

 6 Arrange the chicken slices and the broccoli on plates.

COOKING IN THE OVEN

If you don't have a steamer, you can cook the chicken in the oven. Preheat the oven to 200°C/400°F/gas mark 6. Put the chicken into an ovenproof dish. Half-fill a roasting tin with hot water, then carefully place the dish with the chicken in it into water. Cover the whole roasting tin with foil. Put the tin in the oven, and cook the chicken for 30 minutes.

Rice balls

Rice balls are the Japanese version of sandwiches. They are often put into packed lunches or taken on picnics. In this recipe, the rice balls are made in small bowls.

What you need

200g short-grain rice
400ml water
50g canned tuna
1 onion
½ tbsp granulated sugar
1 tbsp soy sauce

What you do

1 Put the rice into a **colander**. Put the colander under the cold tap, and run cold water through the rice until the water runs clear.

2 Put the rinsed rice into a saucepan, and add 400ml water. Put a lid on the pan. Bring the water to the **boil**, then lower the heat and **simmer** the rice for about 20 minutes, or until it has soaked up all the water.

3 **Drain** the tuna by emptying it into a colander or sieve and letting the liquid drain away.

4 Put the drained tuna into a bowl. Use a fork to break it up into small pieces.

5 **Peel** the skin from the onion and finely **chop** half of it.

6 Put the sugar, soy sauce, and chopped onion into a saucepan.

7 Simmer the mixture until the sugar has **dissolved** and the onion is soft.

8 Add the tuna to the saucepan, and cook for a further 5 minutes.

9 Put 2 tbsp of the cooked rice into a small bowl. Make a hollow in the middle of the rice, and put 1 tsp of the tuna mixture into the hole. Then put another tsp of rice on top and shape the top into a ball with the spoon.

10 Repeat this process until you have used up all the rice and tuna mixture. You should have enough to fill four to six small bowls.

11 Leave the rice balls to **cool**. Serve them in the bowls, or lift them all out onto a large plate.

NORIMAKI

In Japan, rice is often wrapped in seaweed called nori and rolled up. These rolls are called norimaki. To make them, the nori is grilled, the filling is spooned onto it, and it is rolled up into a sausage shape. This is then sliced to make norimaki.

Grilled courgette with ginger

This vegetable dish is simple to make. You could either serve it as a main course or as a side dish.

What you need

2 courgettes
½ vegetable stock cube
1 tbsp soy sauce
½ tbsp granulated sugar
2½ cm piece of fresh ginger
50ml water

What you do

1 With a sharp knife, cut the ends off the courgettes, then cut them in half lengthways.

2 Carefully **peel** the ginger using a sharp knife. Either **grate** or finely **chop** the ginger.

3 Arrange the courgette halves, skin side down, on a grill pan. **Grill** for 5 minutes, until they begin to brown.

4 Turn the courgette halves over, so the skin faces up. Grill for a further 5 minutes.

5 Put 50ml water into a saucepan, and bring it to the **boil**. Crumble half a stock cube into the water, and stir until it **dissolves**.

6 Add the soy sauce and sugar to the stock, and **simmer** for 5 minutes.

7 Place the courgette halves onto plates, then pour the sauce over them.

8 **Sprinkle** the grated or chopped ginger over the courgettes, then serve.

AUBERGINE ALTERNATIVE
You could try making this dish with aubergines instead of courgettes. Cut the aubergines into slices, then grill them for 10 minutes on each side.

Chicken, sesame, and pea salad

Sesame seeds are popular in Japanese cooking and used widely in dishes. They are often **sprinkled** onto sushi and salads and they are found in many baked snacks. The seeds are rich in vitamins, minerals, and healthy fats.

What you need

2 skinless chicken breast fillets

500g baby spinach leaves

200g frozen peas

1 tsp lemon juice

1 tbsp sesame seeds

1 tsp sugar

1 tbsp soy sauce

4 tbsp chicken stock

What you do

1 In a deep frying pan, cover the chicken fillets with water and bring to a gentle **simmer**.

2 **Poach** the fillets for 10 minutes or until cooked.

3 **Drain** the water from the pan and allow the fillets to **cool** slightly.

4 **Slice** the chicken into strips or use your fingers to **shred** it.

5 **Steam** the baby spinach leaves and peas for about 3 minutes, or until tender.

6 Divide the vegetables between four serving plates. Sprinkle the lemon juice over the vegetables and top with shredded chicken.

7 Put the sesame seeds into a frying pan without adding any oil. **Toast** them over a medium heat for about 5 minutes, tossing them occasionally, until they are golden brown. Beware of seeds popping out!

8 Crush the toasted sesame seeds in a mortar and pestle or using a rolling pin on a cutting board.

9 Place the seeds in a mixing bowl Add the sugar, soy sauce, and stock. Stir well and pour over the salads.

Green beans with sesame seeds

Sesame seeds are often used as part of a **dressing** or sauce in Japanese cooking. They go very well with the beans in this recipe.

What you need

100g green beans
1 tbsp sesame seeds
½ tbsp granulated
    sugar
½ tbsp soy sauce
1½ tbsp water

What you do

1. Cut the stalk ends off the green beans, then cut them into pieces 5cm long.

2. Fill a saucepan with water, and bring it to the **boil**.

3. Add the beans, and cook for 2 minutes. **Drain** the beans, and put them into a large bowl.

4. Put the sesame seeds into a frying pan without adding any oil. **Toast** them over a medium heat for about 5 minutes, tossing them occasionally, until they are golden brown. Beware of seeds popping out!

5. Mix the toasted sesame seeds, sugar, soy sauce, and water in a small bowl.

6. Pour the dressing over the beans, and serve.

CABBAGE LEAVES

This sesame seed dressing could be used to dress other vegetables. Try cooking some Chinese cabbage leaves by carefully lowering them into boiling water for about a minute, draining them, then pouring the sesame seed dressing over them.

Toffee sweet potatoes

Traditional Japanese food does not include many desserts. However, Japanese people sometimes eat cakes and other sweet dishes as a snack with a cup of tea (see page 41).

What you need

225g sweet potatoes
75g granulated sugar
50ml water
1 tbsp sesame seeds

What you do

1 **Peel** the sweet potatoes, and **slice** them into pieces about 1½ cm thick.

2 Put the sesame seeds into a frying pan without adding any oil. **Toast** them over a medium heat for about 5 minutes, tossing them occasionally, until they are golden brown. Put the toasted sesame seeds to one side.

3 Put the slices of sweet potato into a saucepan, and cover them with water.

4 Bring the water to the **boil**, then **simmer** the potatoes for 10 minutes, until they are just beginning to go soft.

5 **Drain** the potatoes, and put them on one side.

6 Put the sugar into a pan with 50ml water, and bring the mixture to the boil. Boil it for about 7 minutes, without stirring, until the mixture turns into a light brown **syrup**.

7 Add the cooked sweet potato slices to the warm syrup, turning them so that they are well coated. **Sprinkle** them with the toasted sesame seeds.

8 Put a sheet of **greaseproof paper** onto a plate. Take the potatoes out of the pan, one by one, and lay them on the paper.

9 Leave the potatoes until the toffee syrup hardens.

GREEN TEA

Japanese people drink green tea with everything! Green tea is drunk plain, without milk or sugar. You should be able to find green tea in your local supermarket or delicatessen – why not try drinking it with the recipes in this book?

Japanese lunch box

Lunch boxes, known as *bento*, are very common in Japan. People take lunch boxes to work or school, but they are also sold in railway stations, theatres, and restaurants.

You can put any sort of food into your lunch box, although it is probably not a very good idea to include clear soup! Lunch boxes are a good way of using up any leftovers from your Japanese cooking. Here are some of the recipes in this book you could use:

- grilled tofu (see page 16)
- grilled chicken (see page 18)
- salmon teriyaki (see page 26)
- beef tataki (see page 28)
- steamed chicken with broccoli (see page 30)
- green beans with sesame seeds (see page 38)
- rice balls (see page 32)
- toffee sweet potatoes (see page 40)

Some Japanese lunch boxes also include fresh fruit.

Rolled omelette

Here is a quick and easy recipe that's ideal to go in a lunch box. Make one omelette for each person.

What you need

2 eggs
1 tbsp soy sauce
1½ tsp granulated
   sugar
1½ tbsp sunflower oil

What you do

1 Crack the eggs into a small bowl. **Beat** them with a fork or whisk until the yolk and the white are mixed. Add the soy sauce and sugar, and mix well.

2 Heat the oil in a frying pan over a medium heat. Pour in the egg, and tilt the pan so that the mixture spreads evenly over the bottom of the pan.

3 Cook the omelette for about 5 minutes, until it is set.

4 Tip the omelette onto a chopping board. Wait for it to **cool** for a minute or two. Roll the omelette up into a tube-shape, and leave it to cool for at least 5 more minutes.

5 When it is cool, cut the omelette into **slices** about 2cm thick.

Further information

Here are some places to find out more about Japan and Japanese cooking.

Books

Japanese Cooking for Kids by Kimberly Ono (Elton-Wolf, 2003)

The Second International Cookbook for Kids by Matthew Locricchio (Marshall Cavendish, 2008)

Sushi for Kids: A Children's Introduction to Japan's Favorite Food by Kaoru Ono (Tuttle, 2003)

Tea Ceremony by Shozo Sato (Tuttle, 2005)

The Manga Cookbook by Chihiro Hattori (Japanime, 2007)

A Visit to Japan by Peter and Connie Roop (Heinemann Library, 2008)

Websites

http://web-japan.org/kidsweb/cook/index.html

www.nsknet.or.jp/%7Etomi-yasu/index_e.html

http://japanesefood.about.com/od/sushiforbeginner/a/introtosushi.htm

Healthy eating

This diagram shows the types and proportion of food you should eat to stay healthy. Eat plenty of foods from the *bread, rice, potatoes, pasta* group and plenty from the *fruit and vegetables* group. Eat some foods from the *milk and dairy* group and the *meat, fish, eggs, beans* group. Foods from the smallest group are not necessary for a healthy diet so eat these in small amounts or only occasionally.

Healthy eating, Japan style

Japanese food includes lots of rice and noodles, which is one of the larger sections of the plate. Japanese people also eat a lot of vegetables, some fish, and a little meat. They eat very few desserts, so you can see how healthy Japanese cooking is!

↑ The Eatwell food plate shows the proportion of food from each food group you should eat to achieve a healthy, balanced diet. This takes account of everything you eat, including snacks.

Glossary

beat mix something together strongly using a fork, spoon, or whisk

boil cook a liquid on the hob. Boiling liquid bubbles and steams strongly.

chop cut something into pieces using a knife

colander bowl-shaped container with holes in it, used for draining vegetables and straining

cool allow hot food to become cold. You should always allow food to cool before putting it in the fridge.

cover put a lid on a pan, or foil over a dish

dissolve mix something into a liquid until it disappears

drain remove liquid, usually by pouring something into a colander or sieve

dressing oil and vinegar sauce for salad

fry cook something in oil in a pan

grate break something such as cheese into tiny pieces, using a grater

greaseproof paper kind of paper that does not absorb oil or fat

grill cook something under the grill

humid a climate that is hot and wet

marinate soak something such as meat or fish in a mixture called marinade before cooking, so that it absorbs the taste of the mixture

peel remove the skin of a fruit or vegetable

poach cook something by heating it gently in water or some other liquid

preheat turn on the oven or grill in advance, so that it is hot when you are ready to use it

protein a body-building material found in some foods such as beans, eggs, and meat

pulp a mixture that has been mashed or blended until smooth

rinse wash under a cold tap

shred cut or tear something such as lettuce into small pieces

simmer cook a liquid gently on the hob. Simmering liquid bubbles and steams gently.

slice cut something into thin, flat pieces

sprinkle scatter small pieces or drops on to something

steam cook in steam from boiling water

stir-fry fry something very quickly in a wok or frying pan, stirring all the time

syrup thick, sweet liquid made from sugar and water

toasted heated in a pan without any oil

vegetarian food that does not contain meat or fish. People who don't eat meat or fish are called vegetarians.

Index